This book belongs to

....

Published in 2022 by Welbeck Editions
An imprint of Welbeck Children's Limited,
part of Welbeck Publishing Group
Based in London and Sydney.
www.welbeckpublishing.com

Associate Publisher: Laura Knowles
Commissioning Editor: Bryony Davies
Art Editor: Deborah Vickers
Designer: Ceri Woods
Production: Melanie Robertson

ISBN: 978-1-80338-041-4

Printed in Heshan, China

10 9 8 7 6 5 4 3 2 1

AROUND the WORLD in 80 FESTIVALS

Written by
Nancy Dickmann

Illustrated by
Lucy Banaji

W

WELBECK
EDITIONS

Contents

A world of festivals

Who doesn't like a party? People around the world celebrate thousands of different holidays and festivals. Communities come together to take part and have fun. Some festivals are mainly for families to enjoy at home, while others provide the opportunity for street parties and city-wide celebrations.

What are festivals?

A festival is any event that is celebrated by a community as part of its culture. Many festivals, such as Easter and Diwali, form part of a religion. Others remember loved ones who have died, or historical people and events. Many of these festivals have been celebrated in the same way for hundreds or even thousands of years.

Festival ingredients

Although each festival is unique, there are some common ingredients. For example, they often include the sharing of food and drink—including special foods that might only be eaten during the festival. Traditional costumes often take the place of modern clothes. There may be live music and dancing, and even parades and fireworks!

Just for fun

Many festivals have a serious origin, even if their rituals are joyful and fun. But some modern festivals are just plain silly! There is International Talk Like a Pirate Day on September 19, Star Wars Day on May 4 (a play on "may the force be with you"), and on March 14 people often eat pie. Why? Because the numbers of the date link in with the mathematical number pi (3.14), of course!

Pack your bags

It's time to discover the huge range of holidays and festivals that are celebrated around the world. Some are linked to one particular country or culture, while others have spread to many regions, meaning there are a lot of differences in the way they are celebrated. Are you ready to begin the journey? Then let's go!

The AMERICAS

Do you feel like taking one of the world's longest road trips? You can drive nearly all the way along the Pacific coast of North and South America—but the route is about 30,000 miles long! The Americas are a huge region, with an incredible variety of countries, cultures, and celebrations.

Melting pot

Both continents are rich with indigenous cultures, from the Iñupiaq people of the Arctic circle all the way down to the Mapuche of southern Chile. The Iroquois, Navajo, Maya, Aztecs, Incas, and other groups each built their own civilization, with distinct cultures and traditions.

Everything changed when European explorers arrived, starting in 1492. They brought their own ideas and often conquered the indigenous groups. They also tore Africans from their homes and brought them to the Americas to work as slaves. In addition, millions of ordinary European people came to start a new life. This means that the culture of the Americas is often a mix of indigenous, European, and African.

JUNKANOO

THANKSGIVING

4TH OF JULY

SOYAL

JUNETEENTH

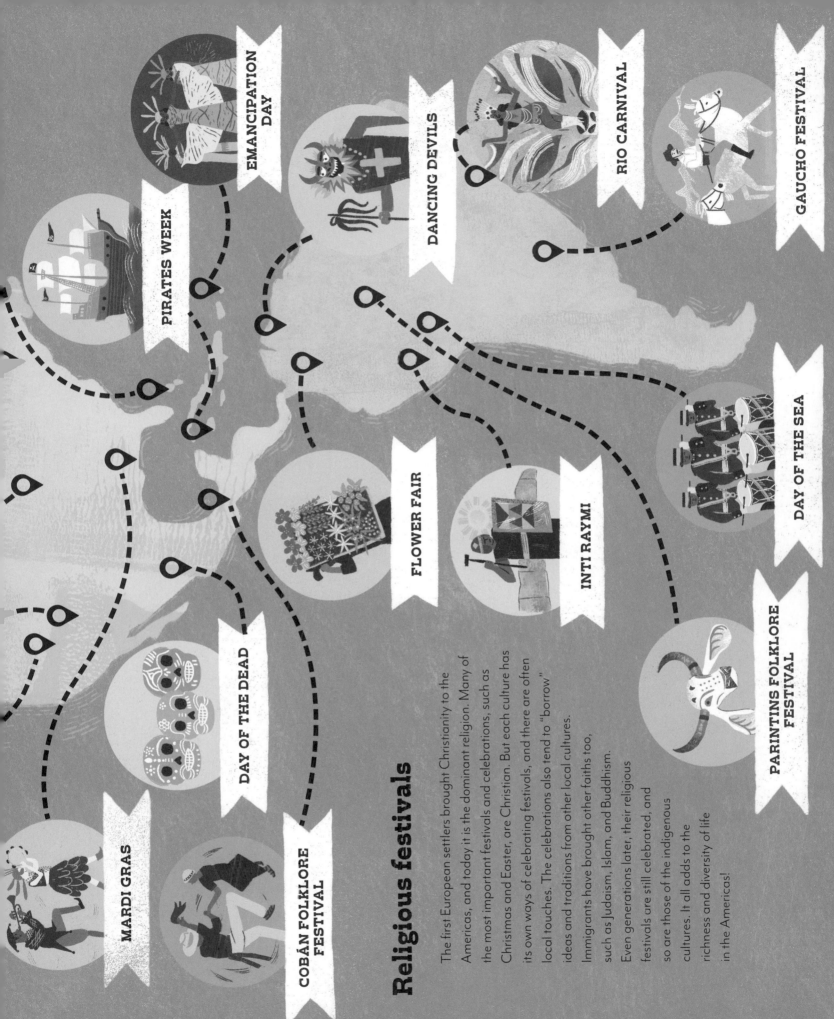

EMANCIPATION DAY

DANCING DEVILS

RIO CARNIVAL

GAUCHO FESTIVAL

PIRATES WEEK

FLOWER FAIR

INTI RAYMI

DAY OF THE SEA

DAY OF THE DEAD

COBÁN FOLKLORE FESTIVAL

MARDI GRAS

PARINTINS FOLKLORE FESTIVAL

Religious festivals

The first European settlers brought Christianity to the Americas, and today it is the dominant religion. Many of the most important festivals and celebrations, such as Christmas and Easter, are Christian. But each culture has its own ways of celebrating festivals, and there are often local touches. The celebrations also tend to "borrow" ideas and traditions from other local cultures. Immigrants have brought other faiths too, such as Judaism, Islam, and Buddhism. Even generations later, their religious festivals are still celebrated, and so are those of the indigenous cultures. It all adds to the richness and diversity of life in the Americas!

1. Dancing Devils

In the Venezuelan town of San Francisco de Yare, celebration of the Catholic feast of Corpus Christi is truly spectacular! People dress as devils in red clothes and grotesque masks and march through town. They sing and dance to the sound of drums until they reach the church. Then they fall to their knees, symbolizing the victory of good over evil. This celebration, called "diablos danzantes" in Spanish, has been going on for nearly 300 years, and it is a mix of African, Spanish, and indigenous cultures.

2. Flower Fair

For ten days every August, the city of Medellín, in Colombia, bursts into color. This is the Flower Fair, a festival to celebrate the people who sell flowers on the city's cobbled streets. These *sillateros* parade through the streets, carrying huge flower arrangements on their backs. Each arrangement is unique, and some use thousands of flowers to form pictures and scenes. The festival also includes musical performances, singing competitions, and sporting events.

3. Inti Raymi

Hundreds of years ago, Peru was ruled by the Inca Empire. Today, Inca culture lives on in the Inti Raymi festival, held each year on the winter solstice—the shortest day of the year. After the solstice the days begin to lengthen so, at this time, the Incas would celebrate their sun god, Inti. Today, Peruvians gather at the ruins of Sacsayhuaman to re-enact the ancient celebration. The sound of panpipes and drums fills the air as people process in brightly colored clothes.

4. Day of the Sea

Once upon a time, Bolivia had a coastline on the Pacific Ocean. Unfortunately, they lost it to Chile after a war in the 1880s. Bolivians have never given up hope of getting it back. On March 23 each year, they celebrate the "Día del Mar," or Day of the Sea. There are speeches and military parades with brass bands. People sing songs about the sea. They even listen to the recorded sounds of waves crashing and seagulls squawking!

5. Gaucho Festival

What do you think of when you hear the word "cowboy"? Most people would picture the American Wild West. but Uruguay has a long history of cowboys too, only there they are called *gauchos*. The week before Easter becomes a festival called "Semana Criolla" in honor of the legendary gaucho culture. People wear boots, ponchos, and cowboy hats and take part in rodeo-style events like lassoing and bronco-busting.

6. Parintins Folklore Festival

Lots of cultures like to retell legends, but in the Amazon region of Brazil, they use it as an excuse for a three-day party! There is a local legend about an ox that was killed and then came back to life. During the festival, two teams compete to tell its story better than their rivals. They use floats, dances, music, and incredible costumes to impress the judges with their version of the legend.

7. Rio Carnival

There are street parties, and then there is the Rio Carnival. This five-day Brazilian festival is an absolute riot of color, music, and excitement! If you are ever in Brazil, it's an experience not to be missed.

In the Christian calendar, Lent is the 40-day period that leads up to Easter. It is a time of prayer and fasting. Parties are definitely not allowed, so in many places people throw a really big one just before the start of Lent. This celebration is often called Carnival, and the carnival in Rio de Janeiro is the most spectacular of them all.

Special schools dotted all over the city teach samba, a traditional Afro-Brazilian style of dance and music. Their dancers spend months building floats, sewing costumes, and practicing for the big event. When Carnival comes, more than 80,000 spectators fill the vast Sambodromo to watch thousands of dancers and musicians strut their stuff. Flamboyant costumes are a must, both for the dancers and the musicians—and sometimes the spectators too!

8. Junkanoo

What do you do on the day after Christmas? It's often a time to relax, play games, and eat leftover turkey. But not in the Bahamas! They hold a fabulous street party called Junkanoo. According to legend, when people still kept slaves in the Bahamas, they gave them three days off at Christmas. To this day, people celebrate by dressing up in elaborate costumes and dancing in street parades, to the sound of horns, bells, and goatskin drums.

9. Pirates Week

If there's one thing the Caribbean is famous for, it's pirates—and in the Cayman Islands they make a point of celebrating that history! Back in the day, buccaneers (including the notorious Blackbeard) would often stop at these islands to take on water and provisions. Today, this festival features music, fireworks, swimming contests, and a float parade. But the main event is a mock invasion, when people in pirate costumes arrive by ship and storm the island. Aaarrrr, matey!

10. Emancipation Day

The end of slavery is celebrated across the Caribbean region. In most countries, festivities are held on or near August 1, the date in 1834 when a law banning slavery in British colonies was passed. People took to the streets to rejoice—a tradition that continues today. In Antigua, the day is marked with *J'ouvert*, a street party that starts in the middle of the night and continues into the next day. There are costumed processions, food stalls, and steel bands.

11. Crop Over

Many countries celebrate harvests, and Barbados is no different. In the 1700s, this island was the world's largest producer of sugar cane, and they celebrated at the end of a successful harvest. Today, Crop Over is a six-week festival of Bajan art, music, food, and culture. The Pic-O-De-Crop contest crowns the best calypso music act of the year, and the finale of the festival is the Grand Kadooment, a carnival parade with bands and costumes.

12. Cobán Folklore Festival

High in the Guatemalan mountains, at the heart of a coffee-growing region, lies the city of Cobán. The people here are rightly proud of the region's Maya heritage. Every August they hold a festival to celebrate Maya culture. There are music and dance performances, as well as traditional foods and crafts. Girls compete to be crowned queen—a title based on their commitment to Maya traditions.

13. Day of the Dead

Do you have an urge to eat a sugar skull, or "bread of the dead" decorated with bone shapes? In Mexico, this is just one way that people celebrate the Day of the Dead. This joyous festival is a celebration of life as well as death. There are skulls and skeletons everywhere, and people honor their loved ones by telling stories about their life, clearing their graves, and leaving offerings such as flowers, food, or candles. Some also dress up as skeletons with painted faces to parade through the streets.

Worldwide celebrations

Festivals like Inti Raymi are specific to a local culture, though people come from around the world to watch the colorful pageantry. Other festivals are much bigger, and are celebrated in many corners of the world. These worldwide holidays may have slightly different versions in different places, but they are all a great way to bring communities together!

Religions around the world

Some festivals are celebrated worldwide because they are linked to a religion that has believers in all parts of the world. Christmas, for example, is celebrated around the world, and even people who aren't Christian often join by giving gifts and sharing a meal with loved ones. The Hindu festival of Diwali and the Muslim celebration of Eid ul-Fitr are also observed around the globe.

Celebrating people, history, and movements

Some worldwide festivals celebrate particular groups of people. For example, most countries have a day to celebrate mothers. It may not be on the same day or observed in the same way, but the idea of honoring mothers cuts across cultures and continents. In many countries there are days to celebrate fathers, grandparents, and siblings too!

Pride is a festival celebrating acceptance and achievements of the LGBTQ+ community, when rainbow-themed parades and parties take place around the world. Historical events are sometimes celebrated worldwide too—such as Remembrance Day, marking the end of World War I. Earth Day, when people show their support for protecting the environment, is observed in over 190 countries.

Love and fools

Some festivals have been spreading around the world for so long that no one really knows how or where they started anymore! A version of April Fool's Day is celebrated in many countries. People play tricks on each other, and newspapers and TV stations put out fake stories to fool people.

Other festivals grow and change over the centuries. Valentine's Day was once a Christian day to honor Saint Valentine. Today it has evolved into a festival of love and romance that is celebrated around the world by Christians and non-Christians alike. They send romantic cards called valentines and give gifts, such as chocolates or flowers, to their special someone.

17

14. Mardi Gras

The Cajuns who live in and around New Orleans use the French name, meaning "Fat Tuesday," for their pre-Lent festival. The motto for this giant street party is *Laissez les bons temps rouler:* let the good times roll. And they certainly do! Revellers in costumes ride through the streets on decorated floats. They throw trinkets to the crowds—often coins or strings of beads in the Mardi Gras colors of purple, green, and gold.

15. Juneteenth

The United States has its own version of Emancipation Day, celebrated on June 19 each year—hence the name "Juneteenth." It dates back to 1865, just after the end of the Civil War, when Union troops landed in Texas on June 19 and announced that all enslaved people in Texas were now free. The date has been celebrated by African American communities ever since then with cookouts, parades, concerts, and parties. In 2021, it became an official national holiday.

16. Thanksgiving

In the first winter after the Pilgrim settlers arrived in Massachusetts in 1620, half of them died. But then the local tribes showed them how to live off the land. After their first harvest the following autumn, legend has it the settlers and the Native Americans sat down together for a feast to give thanks. The original Thanksgiving feast may have included lobster and swan, but today families in the United States and Canada gather to share a meal of turkey and pumpkin pie.

17. Soyal

The Hopi, who live in the deserts of the southwestern United States, mark the winter solstice with a festival called Soyal. It's a time for people to purify themselves and celebrate new life as they lure the sun back from its sleep. Dancers put on masks and costumes to represent spirits called katsinas, who can bring good fortune to the community. These secret rituals are sacred to the Hopi, who have performed them for hundreds of years.

18. Independence Day

In the years after the Pilgrims landed, the new colonies on the east coast were ruled by the British crown. The colonists had to pay taxes, but they had no voice in the British government. As the decades passed, the colonists grew unhappy with the situation. Finally, on July 4, 1776, they declared their independence, but it would take a long and bloody war before the United States of America finally came into being as a country. Now its citizens celebrate their independence every year with elaborate fireworks displays. There are also parades, concerts, and barbecues.

EUROPE

Europe is a relatively small continent, but it packs a lot in. It is densely populated, with bustling cities and many small villages. There is a huge range of different cultures, languages, and traditions. That means there is an enormous variety of festivals as well!

THORRABLÓT

From pagan to Christian

Long ago, most people in Europe were pagan. They might worship many different gods and goddesses, like the ancient Romans and Greeks did, or they might worship nature or ancestor spirits. But once Christianity began, it spread slowly but surely across the continent. In some places, people dropped their old beliefs in favour of the new religion. But many others kept bits of both, and some of the festivals in this chapter have ancient pagan roots.

UP HELLY AA

Other religions

Although Christianity is the largest religion in Europe, there are other faiths too. Islam has spread throughout the continent, particularly in southeastern Europe. Many Jews once lived across Europe, but they have faced persecution throughout history—particularly in WWII, when six million were killed. But their communities, culture, and festivals still live on.

ST PATRICK'S DAY

ST DAVID'S DAY

Crossing borders

In the past, many European countries set up colonies in far-flung corners of the world. Most of these colonies are now independent countries, but their people often emigrate to Europe. The continent also takes in migrants from around the world, and they bring their own festivals and celebrations.

BONFIRE NIGHT

ÓLAVSØKA

GREAT DRAGON PARADE

ST LUCIA'S DAY

ST JOHN'S EVE

OKTOBERFEST

WHITE NIGHTS

FÊTE DE LA MUSIQUE

KURENTOVANJE

VARDAVAR

ANASTENARIA

LA TOMATINA

VENICE CARNIVAL

L-IMNARJA

19. May Day

European winters can be long and harsh, and many countries celebrate the start of spring on May 1. This ancient ritual dates back to pagan times and is a celebration of fertility. In England, people gather flowers and children dance around a tall maypole. A May King and May Queen are crowned, and someone often dresses up as the Green Man, also known as Jack-in-the-Green—an ancient symbol of nature and new life.

20. Bonfire Night

Remember, remember the 5th of November, goes an old nursery rhyme. *Gunpowder, treason, and plot!* In 1605, a plot to blow up the English king and the Houses of Parliament was foiled, and bonfires were lit up and down the country to celebrate this lucky escape. People still light bonfires to burn effigies of Guy Fawkes, one of the bomb-makers. They eat toffee apples and a sticky ginger cake called parkin while watching fireworks displays.

21. St. David's Day

Many countries have a patron saint—a holy person from history chosen to be their special protector. St. David is the patron saint of Wales, and the day of his death is celebrated each year on March 1. People wear the Welsh emblems of leeks and daffodils with pride. Children dress in traditional clothes and perform dances. There are parades and concerts—featuring Welsh songs, of course! It's a day to show your pride in being Welsh.

22. Up Helly Aa

Parts of Scotland were once ruled by the Vikings, including the islands that make up Shetland. People there celebrate their Viking heritage on the last Tuesday of January—in a rather spectacular fashion! Hundreds of people dress up as Viking warriors (they are called "guizers" because they are in disguise) and parade through the streets carrying flaming torches and dragging a replica Viking longboat. At the end of the parade they set it on fire!

23. St. Patrick's Day

In Ireland, March 17 is the day for honoring their own patron saint: St. Patrick, who brought Christianity to the island in about 432 CE. People wear his special symbol, the shamrock, and take part in traditional dancing. The festival started as a religious observance of his life and works, but over the centuries it has changed. Now it is a joyous celebration of Irish culture anywhere in the world where the Irish have settled. It is especially popular in the United States, where Irish communities hold parades and eat food dyed green. In Chicago, they even dye the river green!

Ancient festivals

Some of the festivals we celebrate today, like Mother's Day and Pride, are fairly modern. Others date back centuries, or even more. Humans have been holding festivals for thousands of years. Quite a few of them are still with us, while others have died out.

Roman festivals

The ancient Romans loved a good party and they worshipped a lot of gods and goddesses, so their calendar was jam-packed with festivals. One of the most fun was the topsy-turvy midwinter festival of Saturnalia. Masters and slaves would swap roles, and households would elect a "king" to rule over the celebration. Shops and businesses closed, and there were feasts and gift exchanges.

Celtic celebrations

The Celts who once lived across large parts of Europe had four main festivals that marked the change from one season to the next: Beltane, Imbolc, Lughnasadh, and Samhain. Beltane was a fire festival that marked the beginning of summer. Samhain, at the end of summer, was a time when the world of the gods and spirits overlapped with the human world. The modern festival of Halloween borrows a lot from Samhain.

Around the Mediterranean

The ancient Egyptian new year celebration was called Wepet Renpet. It celebrated the death and rebirth of the god Osiris, as well as the annual flooding of the Nile that made farming possible. The Babylonians celebrated Akitu at the start of spring, reciting poems in honor of the goddess Ishtar. And in ancient Greece, people took part in rites that are still a mystery to this day, to worship the farming goddess Demeter.

All change

Some festivals have been celebrated in the same way for hundreds or even thousands of years. However, others have changed. A lot of celebrations that were originally pagan have been tweaked to align with Christian beliefs and stories. For example, some parts of Saturnalia and the Norse festival of Yule have become part of our Christmas celebrations. Other ancient rituals have been linked to a particular saint or religious holiday. And there are a few festivals, like May Day, which were stopped for a while because they weren't Christian, but have since made a comeback.

24. Thorrablót

If you're curious about trying fermented shark or boiled sheep's head, then this is the festival for you! For centuries, Vikings in Iceland celebrated this midwinter feast in honor of a frost spirit named Thorri. Like many pagan festivals, it died out when Christianity arrived, but was revived again years later. People gather to share traditional Icelandic foods, then follow it with drinking, dancing, storytelling, and playing traditional games.

25. Ólavsøka

The festival of Ólavsøka dates back to the time when the tiny Faroe Islands were part of the Kingdom of Norway. Celebrated on July 29, the day honors Olaf Haraldsson II, a king who became Norway's patron saint after dying in battle. People dress up in Faroese national costume and parade through the streets. The Faroes are so far north that it stays light all night!

26. St. Lucia's Day

The Romans killed St. Lucia in 304 CE, but her feast day is still celebrated in Sweden, over a thousand miles away! One legend says that she brought food to Christians living in hiding, wearing a candlelit wreath to light her way. On December 13, young girls dress in white, wearing wreaths with lighted candles on their heads. (Today, the candles are usually battery-powered, for safety.) At home, they serve coffee, saffron buns, and ginger cookies.

27. Anastenaria

The Swedes may use electric "fire" for safety, but the festival of Anastenaria is much more dangerous! In a handful of villages in Greece and Bulgaria, people walk barefoot across red-hot coals, carrying religious images. Some people say the tradition started when people rescued paintings from a burning church and escaped the flames safely. Others say that it is much older—a ritual designed to honor the ancient Greek god Dionysus.

28. Vardavar

If you don't like getting wet, stay away from Armenia in July. On the Sunday 14 weeks after Easter they celebrate the ancient festival of Vardavar by throwing water on each other! People use buckets, bowls, bottles, and water guns to soak anyone they meet. No one minds because getting splashed is a sign of good luck—and everyone else is just as wet! The festival originally celebrated Astghik, the goddess of water, love, and beauty.

29. L-Imnarja

This ancient Maltese festival takes its name from the Latin word *luminare*, meaning to light up. Today, the celebration on June 28 and 29 honors St. Peter and St. Paul, but its roots go back to the torches and bonfires of the ancient Roman festival of Luminaria. This huge party involves horse and donkey races, a traditional style of folk music called *għana,* and lots of delicious rabbit stew.

30. Kurentovanje

The days before the start of Lent are celebrated in Rio de Janeiro with music and dancing, and in New Orleans with parades and colorful beads. In Slovenia they do it a bit differently—well actually, a *lot* differently. Welcome to Kurentovanje!

In the cobbled medieval town of Ptuj, people dressed as farmers crack bullwhips to clear the streets and make way for hundreds of *kurenti*. These are people dressed as friendly demons who have the power to chase away winter and bring in the spring. The *kurenti* are a truly impressive sight, dressed in hairy suits and huge horned headdresses made of sheepskin.

The cowbells they wear on their belts clang loudly and they carry maces made of hedgehog spikes. Crowds gather to cheer them along as they make their way through the town, creating enough noise to make winter pack up and go away for another year. There's plenty of food and drink to share, including *krofi*—dounuts filled with warm apricot jelly. What a way to welcome the spring!

31. La Tomatina

In the Spanish town of Buñol, the last Wednesday in August marks one of the world's biggest and messiest food fights. It starts with crowds of people trying to pull down the ham attached to the end of a greased pole. Then trucks tip over 100 tonnes of ripe tomatoes into the streets. And the mayhem begins! People hurl tomatoes at each other until a horn sounds an hour later. Then they get hosed down to wash off the sticky pulp.

32. Sant Antoni

Most festivals are for people, but pets get to join in too at the festival of Sant Antoni (St. Anthony) in Spain. He is the patron saint of animals, so people take their pets to be blessed by a priest. There is food—particularly paella—and parades of giant hand-painted wooden figures. On the island of Mallorca, watch out for the *correfoc* or "fire run," where people dressed as devils or animals set off fireworks.

33. Venice Carnival

The city of Venice has celebrated carnival ever since 1162, and the Venetians do it in their own way. Fancy dress—often 18th century finery—and masks are a must. There are elegant masked balls, concerts, carnival rides, and parades of boats on the city's canals. Visitors keep up their energy by eating donuts called *fritelle* and fried pastries covered in icing sugar. The carnival (and the wearing of masks) faded from 1797 and was banned in the 1930s, but it was revived in 1979.

34. Fête de la Musique

They say that that music is a universal language, and a holiday to celebrate it started in France. In 1982, Paris turned into a city of music on June 21, with bands, singers, DJs, and other musicians performing throughout the city to celebrate the joy of music. Now there are thousands of events around the country, and up to 10 million people take part. And over 100 other countries have started celebrating it as well!

35. Il Palio

There are horse races, and then there's Il Palio in Siena, Italy. This frenetic race around the city's main square has been taking place since medieval times. After a ceremonial parade, ten riders representing different neighborhoods of the city mount their horses. They wear old-fashioned costumes and ride without saddles or stirrups. Competition is fierce, and huge crowds pack into the center of the square to watch the jockeys complete three laps. It's over after about one minute of fast and furious action, with cannon fire signalling the end of the race and one rider claiming the coveted silk flag.

36. Great Dragon Parade

According to an old Polish legend, an evil dragon once lived beneath Wawel Castle in the city of Kraków. The king's knights weren't able to kill it, but a clever shoemaker tricked the dragon into eating a fake calf stuffed with burning sulfur. The dragon got such a terrible stomach ache that he rushed to the river, drank too much water, and exploded! Today, this legend is celebrated each June with fireworks and a parade of dragons through the city's Old Town. There are giant puppets, inflatable flying dragons, and even barges that carry swimming dragons down the River Vistula.

Fête de la Musique
June 21

Inti Raymi
June 22

St. John's Eve
June 23

Parantins Folklore Festival
Last weekend in June

L-Imnarja
June 28/29

Juneteenth
June 19

Il Palio
Either July 2 or August 16 (held twice a year)

Crop Over
June to the first Monday in August

Independence Day
July 4

"Three Manly Sports" Festival
July 11-13 in Ulaanbaatar; other dates elsewhere

Coban Folklore Festival
The exact dates change but the festival is in July

JUNE

JULY

Great Dragon Parade
The dates move between late May and early June

White Nights Festival
Late May to late July

Anastenaria
May 21

Counting on nature!

Last, there are a few festivals that aren't based on a calendar at all—at least, not one that you write down on paper. They are scheduled according to the cycles of nature. The **New Yam Festival** is a harvest festival, so it depends on the timing of the rainy season and when the yam harvest is ready. Likewise, **Gerewol** always takes place at the end of the rainy season. In Samoa, the **Rise of Palolo** takes place when the worms rise to the surface to spawn, and this schedule depends on the season and the waning of the moon.

MAY

AUGUST

Cherry Blossom Festival
The dates move between mid-March and early May

Maitisong
The exact dates move but the festival is in April

Coming Together
A moveable date in April

Thai New Year
April 13

Children's Day
April 23

May Day
May 1

Labor Day
May 1

APRIL

Lunar calendars

The calendar you use every day is based on the sun, with a year taking the same time as Earth takes to go once around the sun. But many cultures and religions still use a lunar calendar, which is based on the phases of the moon. Sometimes extra days are added between months to keep it more or less in line with the solar calendar. Lunar calendars are common in Asia. Here are some festivals that are based on lunar calendars:

Dragon Boat Festival
Cheung Chau Bun Festival
Obon
Phaung Daw U Pagoda Festival
Matariki

Vietnamese Lunar New Year
Pushkar Camel Fair
Festival of Light
Holi
Teej

Cow Festival
Festival of the Sacred Tooth
Eid ul-Fitr
Sukkot
Hanukkah

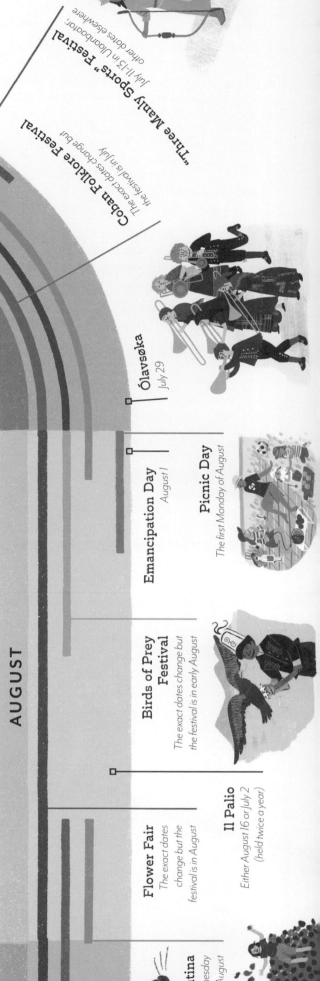

Ólavsøka
July 29

Emancipation Day
August 1

Picnic Day
The first Monday of August

Birds of Prey Festival
The exact dates change but the festival is in early August

Flower Fair
The exact dates change but the festival is in August

Il Palio
Either August 16 or July 2 (held twice a year)

La Tomatina
The last Wednesday in August

SEPTEMBER

Umhlanga Reed Dance
The dates move but the festival is in late August or early Sept

Gorilla Naming Festival
Occurs some time in September

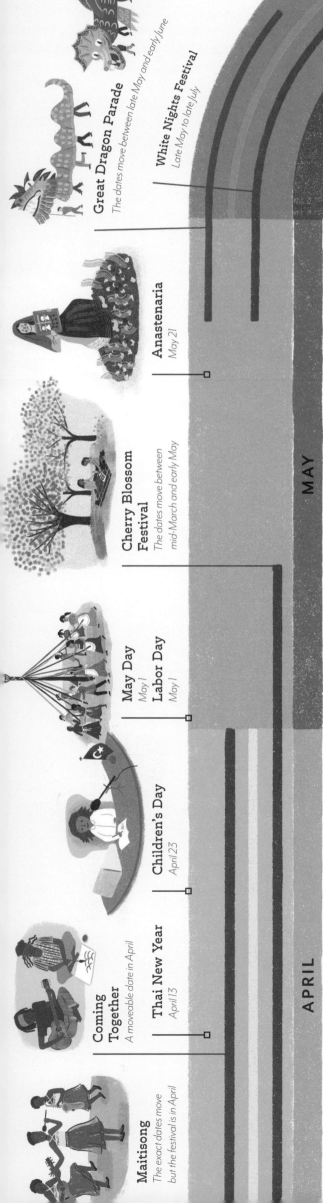

ASIA

Asia is truly immense. It's the largest continent by area, and it's also home to more than half of Earth's population. This enormous land mass stretches from Turkey and the Middle East all the way to the islands of Japan. There are vast forests, arid deserts, huge mountains—and there are plenty of festivals as well!

Religious festivals

Christianity may be the main religion in Europe and the Americas, but the largest faiths in Asia are Islam and Hinduism, with Buddhism not far behind. Many of the festivals celebrated here, such as Eid, Holi, and Esala Perahera, reflect the beliefs of those religions. There are also millions of people who follow folk religions, worshipping nature and ancestor spirits.

Spreading out

People from Asia have emigrated all over the world, bringing their culture with them. For example, many large cities have a "Chinatown" neighborhood where Chinese immigrants have settled. Communities like these continue to celebrate their holidays and festivals. It's a way of keeping a connection to their culture, and it's also a great way to bring their festivals to a wider audience.

World famous

Some Asian festivals may be local to a particular region, but they are now known around the world. Thanks to the internet, people can share pictures and videos of fun and fabulous festivals such as Songkran or Holi. Tourists flock to Asia from other places to join in and create their own memories.

BIRDS OF PREY FESTIVAL

NOWRUZ

CHILDREN'S DAY

PUSHKAR CAMEL FAIR

EID UL-FITR

FESTIVAL OF THE SACRED TOOTH

HANUKKAH

40

Some festivals move around so that they're always on the same day of the week. For example, Picnic Day is on the first Monday of August, and Thanksgiving in the United States is on the fourth Thursday of November. This might be so that the festival always falls on a weekend, or makes it easy for people to have a three or four-day weekend.

Other festivals move because they're based on a different calendar system, such as the Jewish calendar. For users of that calendar system, the festival is always on the same day of the year, but when it's transposed to our usual Western calendar, the date can change. So Hanukkah always starts on the 25th day of Kislev, but that can be any time from late November to late December.

Turn the page to see when in the year the festivals in this book fall.

COW FESTIVAL

"THREE MANLY SPORTS" FESTIVAL

KOREAN ALPHABET DAY

CHERRY BLOSSOM FESTIVAL

FESTIVAL OF LIGHT

HARBIN ICE FESTIVAL

CHEUNG CHAU BUN FESTIVAL

VIETNAMESE LUNAR NEW YEAR FESTIVAL

PHAUNG DAW U PAGODA FESTIVAL

THAI NEW YEAR FESTIVAL

41. Harbin Ice Festival

In northeastern China, for centuries people made hollow ice lanterns to light their way through the bitterly cold winters. Over time these lanterns got fancier, and the region around the city of Harbin became famous for the decorative lanterns. Now the city hosts a festival every winter, where artists come to build the biggest ice sculptures in the world! There is an ice city featuring buildings up to 150 feet tall that visitors can walk inside. At night, the scene is lit by the traditional ice lanterns that started it all.

42. Dragon Boat Festival

Along the Yangtze River, many people in China celebrate a spring festival by staging a boat race. And these aren't just any boats! Their ends are carved to look like the head and tail of a dragon. Teams of rowers paddle them along while one beats a drum to keep everyone in time. The rowers keep their strength up by eating the festival's specialty, dumplings made from sticky rice wrapped in bamboo leaves.

43. Cheung Chau Bun Festival

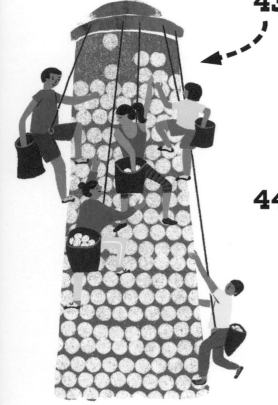

All hail the humble bun! In Hong Kong, a rice-flour bun called a *ping on* is a popular treat. And once a year, the buns take center stage in a wild and colorful festival. There are parades, lion dances, and offerings to the god Pak Tai. But the main event is the bun scrambling contest, where climbers scale an 60-foot tower covered in buns (these days, they're plastic, for safety). The climber who bags the most buns wins!

44. Korean Alphabet Day

The bun festival shows that people can come together to celebrate just about anything. In North and South Korea, they get a day off work to celebrate their alphabet! Long ago, the Korean language was written using Chinese characters. In 1443, King Sejong declared that his people needed their own alphabet, so Hangul was developed. This alphabet is simpler to learn than Chinese, so more people could learn to read. Now that's something worth celebrating!

45. Cherry Blossom Festival

Each spring, Japan's cherry and plum trees burst into glorious blossom. It's time to enjoy the ancient tradition of *hanami*—viewing the beautiful flowers before they fall. For centuries, people have strolled through the trees, writing poems about their beauty. The blossom reminds people that nothing lasts forever, so they make sure to enjoy it while they can. For many people, that means a picnic with friends under the beautiful trees.

46. Obon

When it comes to celebrating festivals, family is important—even when they're no longer with us. In Japan, the Buddhist summer festival of Obon is a way for people to remember their ancestors and welcome them back into their homes.

One legend says that the festival began when one of the Buddha's disciples asked for advice on how to free his mother's spirit from the "Realm of Hungry Ghosts." Buddha suggested making offerings, and that tradition continues today. People across the country return to their hometowns to visit their relatives' graves. They clean them, burn incense, and leave food and other offerings.

In the streets, people perform a folk dance called *bon odori* to welcome the spirits of the dead. They hang lanterns from their houses to guide the dead back home. At the end of the three-day festival, they light bonfires and float lanterns on the river to guide the spirits back to the spirit world.

47. Eid ul-Fitr

For Muslims, the month of Ramadan is a time of prayer and fasting. A festival called Eid ul-Fitr marks the end of Ramadan. It is celebrated by Muslim communities around the world, as families gather to pray and share food. As they go about their day, they greet people with a joyful "Eid Mubarak!," meaning "blessed Eid." In Saudi Arabia, where Islam first began, people bake rose-flavored cookies filled with dates.

48. Nowruz

In the region that was once known as Persia, the new year traditionally starts at the spring equinox. People have celebrated this festival, called Nowruz, for over 3,000 years. There are different celebrations across the region, including sports contests, strolling musicians, and preparation of special foods. Before the festival starts, people light bonfires as a symbol of burning anything bad from the previous year. Some people jump over the bonfires for good luck!

49. Children's Day

What would it be like if children ruled the world? In Turkey, they get a chance to run the country once a year. Kemal Atatürk, the founder of modern Turkey, believed that children were the future of his country. He set aside April 23 as Children's Day. Children receive gifts of candy and toys and take part in singing and dancing performances. The luckiest ones get to sit in Parliament and take over the government for the day!

50. Sukkot

According to legend, when Moses led the Jewish people out of slavery in Egypt, they travelled for 40 years in the desert. To remember how God protected them during this time, Jewish people today celebrate the festival of Sukkot. Each family builds an open-air shelter called a *sukkah* outside their home in memory of the flimsy, temporary shelters in the desert. Families eat in the shelters during the week-long festival, and some even sleep in them!

51. Birds of Prey Festival

People in Kyrgyzstan have been using eagles, hawks, and falcons to hunt for many centuries. They were able to tame these wild birds and train them to bring back prey, such as rabbits, to feed their families. Each August in the village of Bokonbayevo, on the shores of Issyk-Kul Lake, people gather to celebrate this heritage. There are hunting demonstrations as well as traditional games and lots of Kyrgyz food and crafts.

52. Hanukkah

This Jewish festival of lights celebrates an ancient miracle. Long ago, the Jewish people only had enough oil to keep the holy light in their temple burning for a single day. But amazingly, the oil lasted for eight days! Today, people light a candle each day during Hanukkah. They give gifts and eat foods fried in oil, such as donuts and potato pancakes called latkes. Children play a game with a spinning top called a dreidel, trying to win chocolate coins.

Food and festivals

Food and festivals are perfect partners. Many festivals are centered around sharing meals with friends and family. At others, people celebrate outdoors, fuelled by tasty treats from street vendors. And a few—like la Tomatina in Spain—are all about using food to have fun!

Special foods

Some foods are reserved for special occasions and only brought out once a year. For example, pumpkin pie is traditional at Thanksgiving, but rarely eaten at other times of year. In China, people eat pastries called mooncakes at the mid-autumn festival. On Christmas Eve in Bolivia, families eat a traditional meat stew called picana at midnight.

Celebrating local produce

There are some festivals where food takes the spotlight. These often celebrate a food that is produced locally, and the festival is held during the harvest. There is a lemon festival in France, an asparagus festival in Germany, and in Gilroy, California, there's a garlic festival where garlic ice cream is served!

There are festivals to celebrate other types of food, too, such as the annual herring festival in Denmark and the lobster festival in the US state of Maine. There is a vegetarian food festival in Thailand and a street food festival in India. Most of these festivals are local, but Melon Day in Turkmenistan is a national holiday, established to show the country's pride in its famous melons.

Strange but true

A few food-based festivals bend the rules and do things a bit differently. In Lopburi, Thailand, once a year people prepare a huge buffet. But they don't eat it! The food is for the local monkeys, who come to eat as people watch. And in Gloucestershire, England, a local cheese forms the center of an annual event. The cheese is rolled down a steep hill and people chase after it!

53. "Three Manly Sports" Festival

The name of this Mongolian festival, Naadam, translates as "three manly sports," so you might be surprised to discover that there are actually four events—and that women can compete in some of them too! People come from across the country to compete in horse races, archery contests, wrestling matches, and a game that's like a cross between dominoes and tiddlywinks. The festival is a celebration of Mongolia's nomadic culture, with parades, concerts, and plenty of food.

54. Thai New Year Festival

In Thailand, the new year festival of Songkran takes the form of a nationwide water fight. April is one of the hottest months, so most people are happy to be doused or squirted! But this festival also has a deeper meaning. Long ago, people collected water that was used to wash statues of the Buddha, and they used it to bless people. The water at Songkran is still believed to cleanse you of bad luck and give you good fortune for the year ahead.

55. Phaung Daw U Pagoda Festival

The Phaung Daw U pagoda in Myanmar is home to five golden statues of the Buddha. During the yearly festival, four of these statues are taken on a nearly three-week boat tour of the surrounding villages. They ride on an ornate golden barge that is towed along by long canoes powered by up to 100 rowers. The local people have a unique style of rowing—standing upright and using one leg to push the oar.

56. Vietnamese Lunar New Year Festival

In Thailand, they celebrate the new year with water, but in Vietnam, they use fireworks at the Tết festival! The loud noises they make scare off evil spirits that could bring bad luck. In fact, this festival is all about securing good luck for the coming year. People decorate their homes with decorations in red and yellow—the colors of prosperity. It's considered bad luck to wear black or white, get into arguments, or to criticzse someone. This makes Tết a very colorful, happy time!

57. Festival of Light

The Mekong River that flows through Laos is hugely important to the people who live along its banks. Each October they stage a festival called Boun Lai Heua Fai to ask water spirits called *nagas* to bring good luck. Villagers do this by building a boat from bamboo and banana plants, then filling it with candles and offerings. They carry the boat through the streets in a procession to the riverbank, then light candles and say prayers as they send the boat floating away. The sight of hundreds of these boats glowing as they float off down the river is truly spectacular.

58. Pushkar Camel Fair

This fair in northwestern India began as an event for camel and horse traders from across the region to meet and sell their livestock. Today it is an enormous event that draws tourists from around the world. There are carnival rides, acrobats, and snake charmers. Visitors can watch camel races and bathe in the holy waters of the lake. There is even a longest mustache competition (for humans) and a beauty contest for camels!

59. Holi

This Hindu celebration is one of the world's most colorful festivals. Marking the transition from winter to spring, it celebrates the victory of good over evil. People burn effigies of the demon Holika on bonfires. The following day, it's time for fun! People take to the streets, throwing colored powder and water at each other. Everyone ends up absolutely smeared with vibrant color, before cleaning up and visiting family.

60. Teej

For Hindus, the loving marriage of the gods Shiva and Parvati is something to aspire to. The Teej festival celebrates women and marriage, as well as the monsoon rains that bring new growth to the land. Married women fast for 24 hours, and dress in their finest red, green and yellow saris and jewelry, including special bangles. They use henna to paint elaborate patterns on their hands before going out to play on swings hung from trees.

61. Cow Festival

The Nepali festival of Gai Jatra is meant to ease the pain of losing a loved one. Anyone who has lost a family member in the past year leads a cow through the streets. If they don't have a cow, a child can dress as one and join the procession instead. Nepalis believe that cows can guide the souls of the dead to heaven. In spite of all this, Gai Jatra is a joyous festival, with costumes, parades, dancing, and street performances.

62. Festival of the Sacred Tooth

A Buddhist temple in the Sri Lankan city of Kandy guards a sacred relic—one of the Buddha's teeth. Once a year, Buddhists hold a festival called Esala Perahera to honor the holy tooth in the hopes that it will bring good rains. The ten-day festival includes torchlit processions through the streets. Drummers, dancers, and fire-eaters lead the way, followed by dozens of elephants wearing elaborate costumes. The centerpiece of the festival is the appearance of the temple's own elephant, which is richly decorated and carries a replica of the casket holding the sacred tooth.

AFRICA

No one knows where or when the very first festival took place, but there's a good chance that it happened somewhere in Africa. It was here that the first humans evolved, about 300,000 years ago. Over time, our species spread to the other continents.

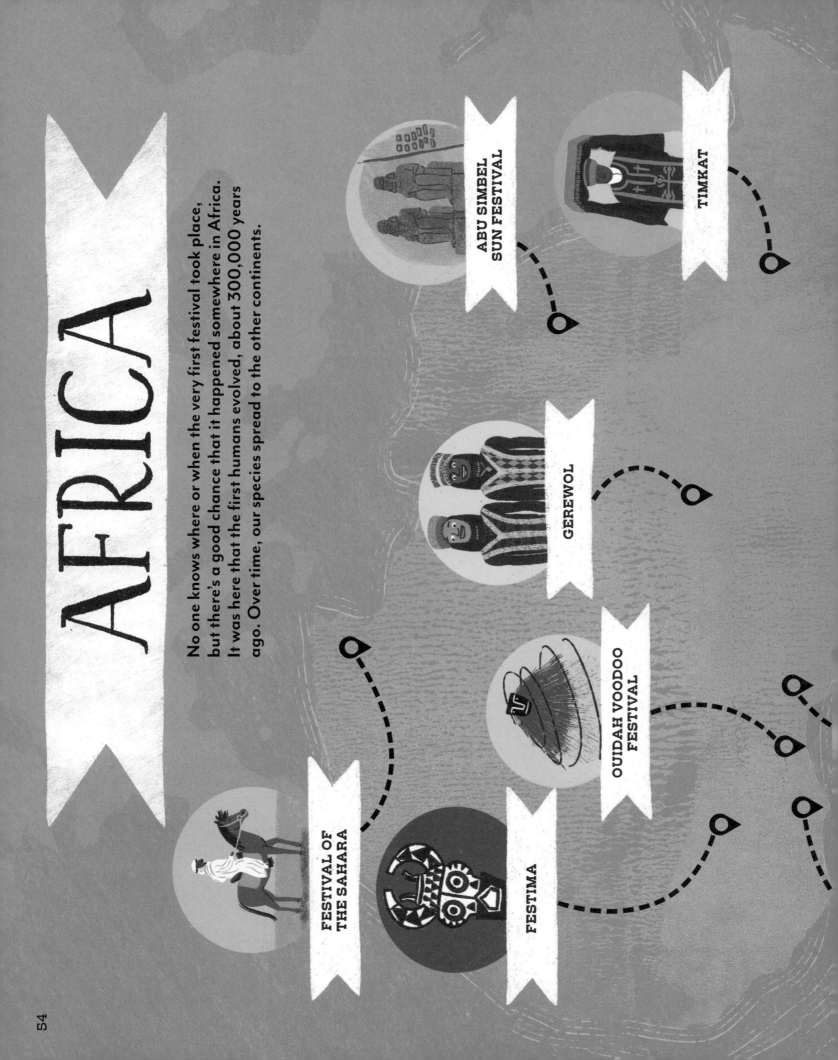

ABU SIMBEL SUN FESTIVAL

TIMKAT

GEREWOL

OUIDAH VOODOO FESTIVAL

FESTIVAL OF THE SAHARA

FESTIMA

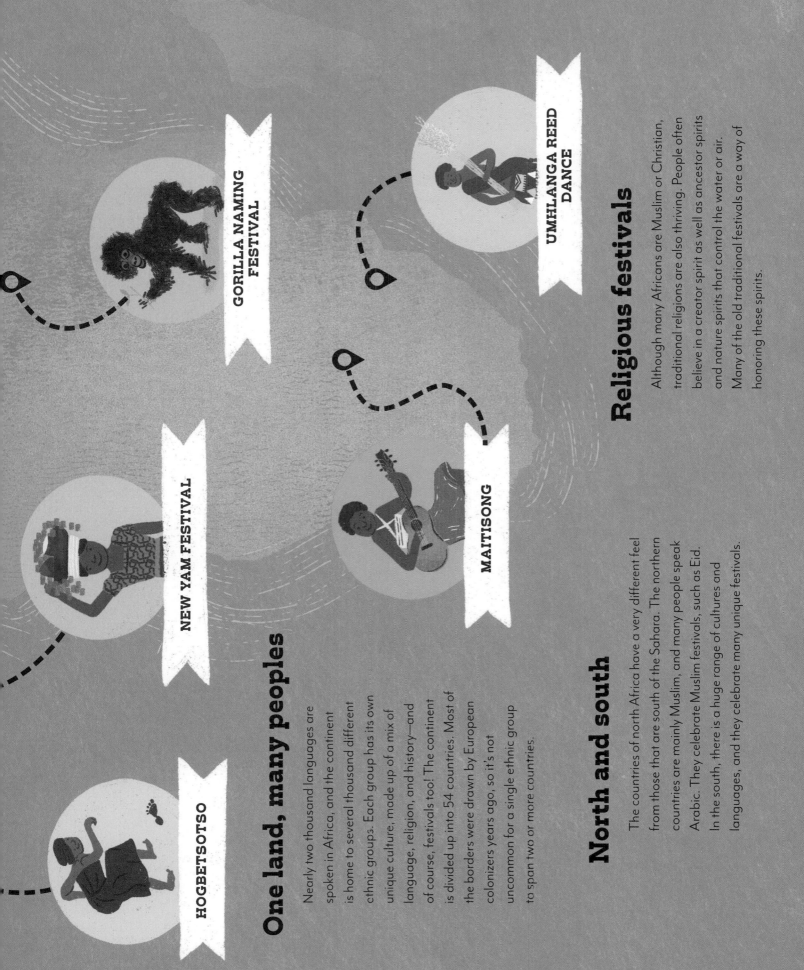

HOGBETSOTSO

NEW YAM FESTIVAL

GORILLA NAMING FESTIVAL

MAITISONG

UMHLANGA REED DANCE

One land, many peoples

Nearly two thousand languages are spoken in Africa, and the continent is home to several thousand different ethnic groups. Each group has its own unique culture, made up of a mix of language, religion, and history—and of course, festivals too! The continent is divided up into 54 countries. Most of the borders were drawn by European colonizers years ago, so it's not uncommon for a single ethnic group to span two or more countries.

North and south

The countries of north Africa have a very different feel from those that are south of the Sahara. The northern countries are mainly Muslim, and many people speak Arabic. They celebrate Muslim festivals, such as Eid. In the south, there is a huge range of cultures and languages, and they celebrate many unique festivals.

Religious festivals

Although many Africans are Muslim or Christian, traditional religions are also thriving. People often believe in a creator spirit as well as ancestor spirits and nature spirits that control the water or air. Many of the old traditional festivals are a way of honoring these spirits.

63. Festival of the Sahara

This annual festival, held in the desert oasis of Douz, Tunisia, started out as a camel festival. Over time, it has become a celebration of nomadic desert culture. There are horse and camel races, of course, but that's not all. The festival also includes falconry demonstrations and traditional poetry, dance, and music. And if you get hungry, there are always dates to eat —in Douz, palm trees outnumber people by 25 to 1!

64. Abu Simbel Sun Festival

The Egyptian pharaoh Ramses II ordered a temple to be built at Abu Simbel, with its entrance guarded by four enormous statues of him. The temple is aligned so that twice a year, the sun shines directly through the narrow entrance. This lights up statues of the gods in an inner chamber. Even today, more than 3,200 years later, people still gather to watch the sun arrive. Afterwards they go into the temple courtyard to share food and watch dancing.

65. Ouidah Voodoo Festival

The voodoo religion originated in the region that is now Benin. Once a year, people come to the coastal town of Ouidah for the world's largest voodoo festival. It's a religious celebration that honors the voodoo gods and shows pride in the local culture. People dress in elaborate, colorful clothes and masks and take part in processions, accompanied by the sound of drums.

66. New Yam Festival

Yams are an important crop for Nigeria's Igbo people, and the harvest is a great excuse for a celebration. In fact, you're not allowed to eat any of the new yams until the festival has taken place! People gather together to give thanks to God and the farmers for a good harvest. Then it's time for a party, with dancing, singing, and fun. People wear colorful traditional clothes and play music on drums and other instruments.

67. Gerewol

Chad's Gerewol festival is a beauty pageant with a twist—the men are the contestants and the women judge them. It's an important event for the nomadic Wodaabe people who live in this harsh, dry landscape. They travel in small family bands, and this festival at the end of the rainy season is the only time they gather together as a large group. Young unmarried men paint their faces red, with white dots and black lipstick. They try to emphasize how white their teeth and eyes are, hoping to attract a wife. Dressed in their finest, the contestants link arms to dance in long lines before the judges.

Dressing up

Festivals are special times, and special times often require special clothes. It may be as simple as a Christmas sweater, or as fancy and fabulous as a sequined carnival costume. Whatever the occasion, festivals are a time for looking your best!

Special meanings

At some festivals, people wear traditional clothes. These are styles that were commonly worn in the past, but are no longer worn in everyday life. Wearing them at festivals is a way for people to celebrate their culture and history. Some clothes that are worn at celebrations have special meanings. Kente is a patterned, hand-woven cloth from Ghana that is often worn on special occasions. Each color and design has its own meaning.

Make your own

The furry suits and horned headdresses worn at the Slovenian festival of Kurentovanje are made by specialist craft workers, but people often sew their own festival costumes. They might use silk and rich brocade fabric, or sew on crystals or even gems. In Brazil, stitching thousands of beads and sequins onto a carnival costume can take months. In the Bahamas, people keep it simple and sustainable by using cardboard, newspaper, and crepe paper to create elaborate costumes for Junkanoo.

Completing the look

Clothes are just part of the package when it comes to creating a festival look. Masks are worn at the Venice Carnival to create an air of mystery—and to give people the confidence to really let their hair down! At many African festivals, masks have a different purpose. They might represent ancestors or animal spirits. Makeup often has an important role, too. At the Gerewol festival in Chad, men paint their faces in traditional patterns. In many cultures, face painting is a way of showing your status, and separating tribe members from outsiders.

68. FESTIMA

Once every two years, the city of Dédougou in Burkina Faso turns into an otherworldly realm, filled with horned demons, brightly colored animals, and human figures covered in leaves. This is FESTIMA (short for Festival International des Masques et des Artes)—an international festival celebrating the ancient tradition of mask-wearing in African culture.

People come to Dédougou from all over West Africa, bringing masks and costumes unique to their ethnic group. The masks, made of wood, straw, leaves and cloth, have been used as part of ancestor worship for many centuries. At FESTIMA, the identity of the person behind the mask is kept secret.

People believe that the masks have magical powers, and when a person wears one while dancing during a ceremony, they can communicate with their ancestors or other spirits. Watching the performances is a great way for these communities to pass on their culture and heritage to the next generation.

69. Hogbetsotso

According to legend, the Ewe people of Ghana were once under the rule of a wicked chief. They managed to escape from his walled city by walking backward so that the direction of their footprints would confuse anyone who tried to chase them. The annual Hogbetsotso festival remembers this courageous journey. People start by ending all disputes and cleaning the town. They pay homage to their chiefs before breaking out the drums and music for dancing and merry-making.

70. Umhlanga Reed Dance

Eswatini's annual Reed Dance is a truly amazing spectacle. Up to 40,000 girls and young women take part, moving in long columns across the land. They march to the reed-beds to cut long reeds, then carry their bundles to the royal residence. Dressed in bright costumes, they dance their way over to present the reeds to the queen mother. The king joins them the following day for more dancing. The entire festival takes eight days.

71. Maitisong

Maitisong is Botswana's biggest arts festival. Local talent and international guests come together in the capital city of Gaborone for a month-long extravaganza of music, dance, poetry, theater, and comedy. There is a special focus on young performers, with two weeks devoted to schools and children. The goal of the festival is to give the local arts scene a chance to inspire the public, and to launch the careers of Botswana's most talented performers.

72. Gorilla naming festival

Rwanda is famous for the rare and endangered mountain gorillas that live there. This festival, called Kwita Izina, meaning "to give a name," is all about the need to protect these majestic creatures. The highlight of the week is a naming ceremony for the baby gorillas born in the park over the last year, which is based on the traditional naming ceremonies for human babies. On a huge bamboo stage shaped like a gorilla, people assign each gorilla a carefully chosen name.

73. Timkat

For many Christians, the festival of Epiphany remembers the baptism of Jesus. In Ethiopia, this festival takes a uniquely African slant and is called Timkat. Priests carry replicas of the Ark of the Covenant on their head in a procession through the streets, while other priests hold decorated umbrellas to shade them. They are followed by thousands of people, all singing and clapping. Many of the pilgrims wear white robes as they follow the processions to the holy pools. Once a priest blesses the water, they jump in to renew their commitment to their faith. There are candlelit prayers as well as feasting, singing, and dancing.

OCEANIA

Looking at Earth from space, you see vast blue expanses. These are the world's oceans, and they cover about 70% of the planet's surface. The islands sprinkled amongst the waters are home to a vast array of peoples and cultures. Many of them are in the Pacific, in a region known as Oceania.

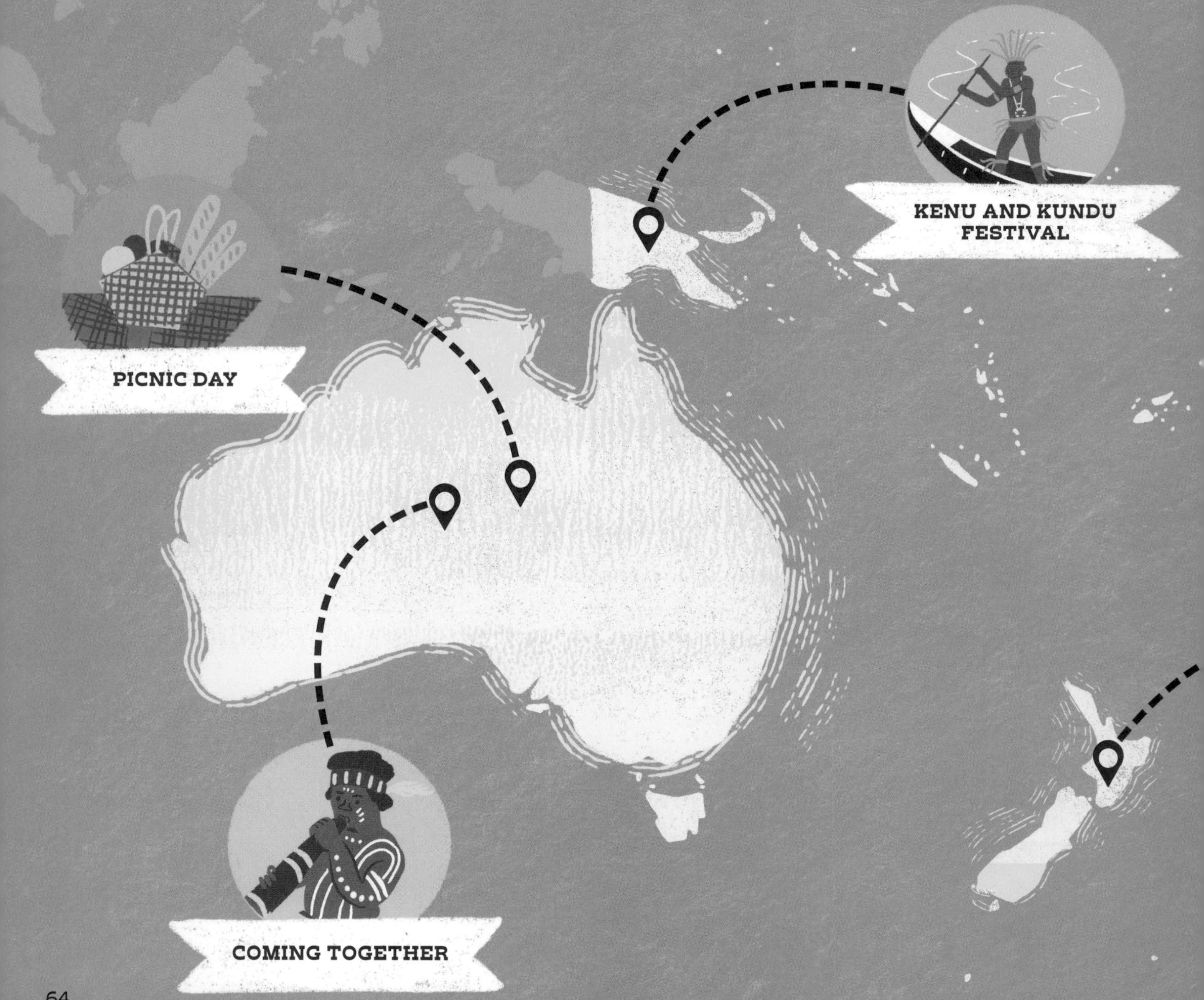

KENU AND KUNDU FESTIVAL

PICNIC DAY

COMING TOGETHER

MERRIE
MONARCH

Ancient sailors

To settle these far-flung islands, ancient people
needed boats. Using dugout canoes, they sailed
from one island to the next, spreading their
culture and their beliefs. Although each island
group has its own unique culture and traditions,
they share a lot with their oceanic neighbors.

RISE OF PALOLO

All change

Life in some parts of Oceania changed with
the arrival of European settlers. Indigenous
people were sometimes pushed aside, and
their traditions sidelined. Today, many of these
cultures are reclaiming their heritage, and
traditional festivals are on the rise. They help
the local economy by attracting tourists, and
they also provide a way for indigenous people
to celebrate their history and culture.

Big and small

The largest land mass in Oceania
is Australia, which is too big to
be an island—it's a continent.
Just down the scale are the large
islands of New Zealand and
Papua New Guinea. Many of the
thousands of other islands are
much smaller. Some are delicate
ring-shaped coral reefs called
atolls, while others are volcanic.

TAPATI
RAPA NUI

MATARIKI

74. Coming Together

In the local Anangu language, Tjungu means "coming together" and, well, that's pretty much the definition of a festival, isn't it? Once a year, Australia's indigenous peoples come together for a celebration of their way of life. First taking place in 2014, this is one of the country's newest festivals—but also one of the most vibrant. In the shadow of the massive red sandstone rock formation known as Uluru, indigenous Australians show off the best of their culture. From music and dance performances to traditional foods and even a mini-film festival, there is something for everyone to enjoy.

75. Picnic Day

Who doesn't love a picnic? In Australia's Northern Territory, the first Monday in August is a public holiday, set aside for doing exactly that. Many people meet up with friends and family for an al fresco feast and an afternoon of sack races and tug-of-war. Others head into the desert for the Harts Range annual race meeting. This includes traditional bush contests like whip cracking, lizard races, horse races—and even a dance!

76. Matariki

Matariki is the Māori name for the small cluster of stars that astronomers know as the Pleiades. In New Zealand, Matariki first rises above the horizon in midwinter. The Māori celebrate this as their traditional new year. It is a time to remember those who have died in the past year, celebrate the present, and plan for the future. Families and communities gather to share food, light fires, make offerings, and tell stories. In 2022, it became an official public holiday in New Zealand.

77. Merrie Monarch

Hawaii is now part of the United States, but not so very long ago it was an independent Polynesian kingdom. Its last king, David Kalākaua, was known as the "Merrie Monarch." He loved the traditional Hawaiian dance called the hula, and he made the ukulele popular as a way to accompany it. Today, this week-long festival honors his commitment to traditional Hawaiian culture. There is a hula competition, a parade, and an art show.

78. Tapati Rapa Nui

Every February, the people of Easter Island—also known as Rapa Nui—stage a contest to choose a ceremonial queen for the year. Each team earns points by taking part in traditional activities. These include traditional crafts as well as sports like canoeing, horse racing, and bodyboarding. The most extreme event is the "Haka Pei," in which competitors slide down an extremely steep hill, using the trunks of banana plants as a sledge.

79. Rise of Palolo

The humble yet delicious palolo worm lives in the reefs that surround the islands of Samoa. Every October, the waning of the moon tells the worms that it is time to spawn. They float to the surface, where they are caught in nets by local people who have been waiting all year for this "palolo rise." Working in small groups, they stand waist-deep in the darkness as they catch the blue-green worms. By the time dawn breaks over the ocean, the worms have left. But the Samoans can enjoy their catch, either raw, fried in butter, or baked into bread.

80. Kenu and Kundu Festival

For the people who live on the islands dotted around the South Pacific,
boats are extremely important. So it's no surprise that this festival
in Papua New Guinea is all about boats (*kenu*) and drums (*kundu*)!
People arrive by canoe from the islands all over Milne Bay. There are
war canoes, trading canoes, and even ones with sails. The rowers
dress in feathers and shells, and when the race begins, they paddle
as one, kept in time by the steady beat of the drums. After the racing
finishes, there is singing and dancing—and plenty of food!

Marking the year

Have you noticed any patterns to the festivals in this book? Although each one is unique and they all reflect the local culture, there are a few ideas and events that keep cropping up. In fact, a lot of the festivals are celebrating more or less the same thing!

Cycles of life

Many festivals are based around the passing of the seasons. People everywhere have always paid close attention to the weather and seasons, because they affect the food supplies that people depend on for their survival. So it's natural that they should inspire a lot of festivals! There are harvest festivals, like Thanksgiving and the New Yam Festival. There are midwinter festivals to celebrate the return of the sun and there are midsummer festivals like St. John's Eve.

New year, new you

Other festivals mark the start of a new year, though they take place at different times, depending on the calendar system you're using. New Year is a great excuse for a party, but the meaning is often deeper than that. People take the opportunity to sweep away any bad memories from the old year and hope for better times ahead. After all, the new year will be full of festivals to celebrate!

Time to celebrate!

Our journey has come to an end, and you're now an expert on lighting candles, throwing water at people and jumping over bonfires. So . . . what's the next step?

Sharing festivals

Which festivals are important to you and your family? Do any of them appear in this book? Next time one of them comes around, perhaps you'd like to share it with your friends. You can explain the meaning of the festival and the traditions that surround it. Maybe you could work together to prepare food, costumes, and decorations, or learn a traditional dance. Sharing festivals is a great way for people to come together and pass on traditions.

Trying something new

Maybe you'd like to experience one of the other festivals in this book. You might have friends who already celebrate it! If not, there may be people in your local area who do. Ask around and you'll likely find a way to take part. Some festivals involve street parties or parades, and all are welcome—just remember to be respectful of other cultures' traditions. You're sure to have a fantastic time!

Index